PETER NAYLOR

W0010159

Discovering
Dowsing and Divining

SHIRE PUBLICATIONS LTD

ACKNOWLEDGEMENTS
The cover design is by Ron Shaddock. The line drawings are by Michael
Stringer. The diagrams are by the author.

Published in 2004 by Shire Publications Ltd, Cromwell House, Church
Street, Princes Risborough, Buckinghamshire HP27 9AA, UK. Website:
www.shirebooks.co.uk
Copyright © 1980 by Peter Naylor. First published 1980; reprinted 1987,
1991, 1993, 1997, 2000 and 2004. Number 251 in the Discovering series.
ISBN 0 85263 516 8.

Printed in Great Britain by CIT Printing Services Ltd, Press Buildings,
Merlins Bridge, Haverfordwest, Pembrokeshire SA61 1XF.

Contents

1. Introduction   5

2. How to begin dowsing   9

3. Other methods of dowsing   17

4. Some advanced techniques   29

5. If you are not successful   32

6. Other applications   33

7. Conclusion   35

Further reading   36

Organisations and equipment   37

Index   38

1. *Divining for metals, a sixteenth-century engraving from 'De Re Metallica'.*

1. Introduction

Most people have heard of dowsing or divining. Some have attempted to do it, without success; some have succeeded but have been none the wiser as a result. This book sets out to show how it is done and, it is hoped, to prove that, contrary to popular opinion, most people can dowse.

By dictionary definition there is no difference between dowsing and divining, but for the purpose of this book 'dowsing' is used for the practical aspect, 'divining' for the interpretation of the results.

Dowsing has been practised for centuries and is practised still as a method of finding water, minerals, pipes, cables and the like. Indeed it is growing in popularity, and professional dowsing is enjoying a revival. Stories about famous exploits in dowsing are legion, and, whilst allowance must be made for flights of fancy, they tell of remarkable achievements.

The written history of dowsing is brief and fairly recent. Dowsing was shrouded in secrecy for centuries, possibly because it was associated with the occult. The earliest written record which may refer to dowsing is in the Bible (Exodus, chapter 17, verse 6): 'and thou shalt smite the rock, and there shall come water out of it, that the people may drink.'

Dowsers appear on ancient Egyptian bas-reliefs and on a statue of the Chinese emperor Kwang Su, about 2200 BC. One of the earliest known illustrations of a working dowser is found in the *De Re Metallica* by Agricola, a treatise on mining and metallurgy first published in 1556. This shows a Saxon searching for mineral veins, using a forked twig as a dowsing rod. He is holding the rod incorrectly, a common fault with beginners, but, if one allows for artistic licence, it is a very fine illustration of a dowser.

The chief source of information about dowsing has been France, mostly from the researches and writings of priests. This is something of a paradox, as the church has consistently condemned dowsing until modern times. The earliest known attempt at explaining the art was by a French abbé, de Vallemont, in the seventeenth century. At about the same time Baron de Beausoleil had recorded that German miners used rods to find mineral veins. It is clear that circumstances had not changed since Agricola two hundred years previously.

Suggestions were being made as early as 1750 that there might be a connection between dowsing and electricity. This theory, further expanded by a Doctor Thouvenal, has been supported over the ensuing years by several scientists and is popularly held today. In 1853 the Academie des Sciences of France appointed a commission to look into the workings of the rod. The findings of this commission were interesting and divided. The ecclesiastical element attributed the workings of the rod to an act of the devil.

In England, a book was published in 1894 by three members of the Mullins family of Wiltshire. It describes their success and lists their patrons, including many of the local landed gentry. The list of successes makes impressive reading, even if it is somewhat boastful. However, if one allows for their exaggerations, the list is nevertheless a formidable one.

During the twentieth century the art came into the open, partly because of a lively scientific interest by learned men and a quiescent attitude on the part of the church.

Unfortunately even today, as over the centuries, there is a widely held belief that dowsing is an agency of the devil, and akin to mysticism. This is not so. It is a purely scientific phenomenon, which can be used equally well by the saintly as by sinners.

There are three popularly held misconceptions about dowsing. The first is that dowsing is a unique gift, given only to the few. This book will demonstrate that it is highly probable that the reader will be able to dowse. Secondly, it is believed by many that dowsing is only for discovering underground springs of water. But it can be used for finding anything that is under the surface of the earth.

The third misconception is that only hazel twigs can be used as dowsing rods. Other twigs can be equally effective, as can bent wires, pendulums, whalebone and other unlikely objects.

The belief that dowsing is a rare gift probably arose from the professional dowser's wish to guard his own livelihood – an early form of restrictive practice. Every village had its dowser, who enjoyed a useful income from his activity, along with a certain prestige. He would have been jealous of his ability and would be reluctant to pass his skill on to others, apart from his eldest son. This gave credence to the belief that dowsing ran in families. It is true that if you tell a novice that he cannot and never will dowse the chances are that he never will.

The author often gives talks and demonstrations of dowsing and he encourages the audience to try it. He has found that, within half an hour, more than eight out of ten of those present, who have never tried before, can undertake elementary dowsing.

The use of dowsing to find minerals in Britain probably outweighed its importance in finding water, which has never been a problem until modern heavy demands for supplies. Finding minerals has been more difficult. The veins are usually vertical or nearly so, and they are hidden by topsoil and vegetation. The use of dowsing to find such veins was very important to the miner and the local community, for frequently the local economy was totally dependent on mining, as in Cornwall and parts of the Pennines.

Dowsers are still in demand, to fill the gaps where modern technology has failed. Dowsing has proved to be more accurate and capable of greater depth than modern search devices such as those used by treasure hunters and statutory undertakings. Some enthusiasts are applying the technique on prehistoric sites, the controversial ley lines and old trackways.

The general reader, however, should treat the subject with light-hearted seriousness, considering dowsing to be a genuine form of ancient technology, but practised for fun and entertainment. This book is an introduction to an old art which is enjoying renewed popularity.

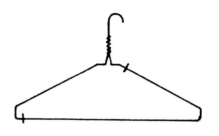

wire coat hanger - stage one

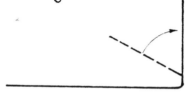

stage two

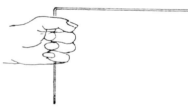

hand held

sleeve

2. Constructing bent metal rods from coat hangers.

2. How to begin dowsing

The easiest way of starting dowsing is to use bent metal rods, on any patch of land, preferably in total privacy. Bent metal rods are easily and cheaply available, reactions can be found in any place and the novice is easily distracted by spectators, particularly if there are sceptics amongst them.

Selection and preparation of the rods

The dowser should select two thin round metal rods, similar to those illustrated in Fig. 2. Each of the rods should be bent into an L shape, one limb being approximately 40 centimetres (16 inches) long, the other limb about 15 centimetres (6 inches) long. The shorter limb is the handle and the longer one the arm. The diameters of the rods should be equal and no more than 2 millimetres (a twelfth of an inch). The type of metal is unimportant. The rods can be cut from metal coat hangers of the type given away at dry cleaners, oxyacetylene welding rods, fencing wire and such like. They need cost nothing. By preference they should be a matching pair, of the same size, diameter and metal. This is less important to the more experienced dowser, but the novice should start with a matching pair.

Attitude

The attitude of the dowser, both physical and mental, is important. Place yourself at random in a field (the back garden will do) and relax. Comfortable clothing helps, and it might be advisable to empty your pockets of metallic objects, such as keys and coins. Ladies should not carry a handbag.

When you are fully relaxed, hold the rods, one in each hand, so that the handles are held in loosely clenched fists. Your arms and those of the rods should point to the ground. Your thumbs should rest on the fingernails of the forefingers (Fig. 3). With the rods hanging loosely at your sides, they should swing freely if the hands are moved.

Now raise your forearms by bending the elbows, which should be kept close to the trunk of your body. The forearms should be held horizontally, with the arms of the rods also horizontal and the handles vertical. Ideally the arms of the rods and the forearms should be in line and perfectly horizontal, on the same plane and parallel with each other (see Fig. 3).

First attempts

In this posture move forward slowly, taking short but firm steps. Resist the temptation to look at the rods; look ahead as if riding a bicycle. You will be aware of the rods moving. Sooner or later, and probably sooner than you would have imagined, the rods will

3. *Dowsing with bent metal rods. The rods should be held horizontal to the ground.*

4. The rods react by crossing as shown, or by opening out to form a V with an open base.

move involuntarily. They will either cross, one over the other, or open out to form a V with an open base. This is the right or left handedness in dowsing, and it is not related to one's own right or left handedness in normal usage.

If you are a novice, you have now made your first dowsing reaction, and it will be a most unusual sensation. Repeat this exercise in different places until you get accustomed to the rods reacting and until the novelty of it begins to wear off a little.

The next stage is to walk over the point of reaction and beyond. The rods should revert to their original position. Keep walking and with practice you will find that the rods will react and revert many times, giving reaction points at intervals. These intervals will vary in distance.

Experimentation

Having got the feel of dowsing with the rods, you should now progress to determining the reaction. This can be accomplished in two different ways, and you should try both.

The first method is to determine the approximate location of a line of reaction by making a few passes over it. With this line fixed in your memory, walk over it in a zigzag, adopting a meandering path, so that the line is crossed and recrossed. Each time the line is crossed a reaction should occur, followed by a reversion to normal.

The second and quicker method is less tiring. Walk along the supposed line of reaction, somewhat like a tightrope walker, having walked on to it from adjoining neutral ground. The rods should remain crossed (or opened) while on the line and will revert when you stray off the line. If the rods remain in the position of reaction it is advisable to check them. This is easily done by stopping and taking a step either side. As you do this, the rods, having moved away from the influence, should revert to normal.

At this stage it will be helpful to enlist a sympathetic friend to assist you. Make some markers – old meat skewers with paper, stones or wooden pegs for example – but nothing that might blow away in the wind. The helper should follow closely behind you, marking the ground below each reaction. After a while the markers will prescribe a fixed pattern of lines of reaction (see Fig. 5). Please remember to remove these markers afterwards, and please observe the country code.

With dowsing, as with all things, practice makes perfect. Your reactions strengthen with usage, and different, previously unknown reactions occur. You will also be able to quicken your pace to a brisk walk. It has been known for dowsers to operate from the passenger seat of a vehicle and even from a light aircraft.

A further refinement could be applied should the dowser

12

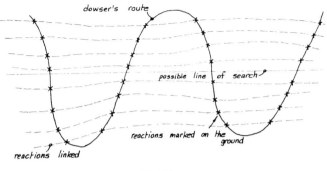

dowser's route

possible line of search

reactions marked on the ground

reactions linked

MEANDERING SEARCH

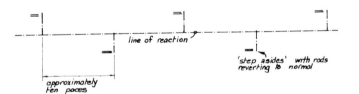

line of reaction

'step asides' with rods reverting to normal

approximately ten paces

WALKING THE LINE

5. Methods of plotting reactions.

experience difficulties with the rods swaying about, particularly if there is a breeze. When there is a strong wind dowsing by rods becomes almost impossible. Try exerting a little pressure on the handles of the rods by gripping them lightly between the thumb and forefinger. With practice you will find that the rods will still move and react but will not give spurious movements.

At the opposite extreme, some people find that the knuckles restrain the rods from moving at all. This happens particularly with people who have prominent knuckles or suffer from arthritis of the hands. It is easily countered by making secondary handles in the form of tubes that will fit over the rods. Ideal for this purpose are cheap ballpoint-pen cases, the stopper and refill having been removed and discarded. These should be held so that the arms of the rods rest on the plastic of the handles and are free to move (see Fig. 6). With this method, however, the rods have no restraint unless a little pressure is applied by the thumb.

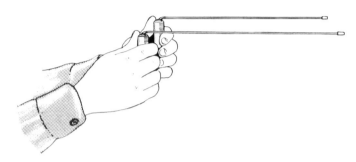

6. *Commercially produced dowsing angle rods which swivel freely within the hand-held sleeves.*

Determining results

Interpreting the results is by far the most difficult part of dowsing and by definition in this book it is known as divining. Having walked the ground and determined lines of reaction, the amateur dowser is naturally interested to know what, if anything, he has found. Left to its own devices, a dowsing rod will react to anything that is underground, from rocks to rivers.

The problem becomes less difficult if it is approached from a different angle. Consider it as 'what am I looking for' rather than 'what have I found'. The professional dowser concentrates very hard on what he is looking for and, it is hoped, finds that substance to the exclusion of all others. If he thinks of water, the rods react to water. This does not always happen, as when the dowser is looking for something with a weak reaction, such as an old foundation, the powerful influence of water will still exert itself. A professional, however, can tell the difference. The amateur cannot be so fortunate as to attain this degree of skill without many years of practice. Even then it is not absolutely reliable and is very exhausting.

The favoured method is to use samples, and this is the easier method for the novice to try. The principle is to carry in one hand a sample of the substance being sought. This sample does the thinking for you. It should be in contact with both the skin of the dowser and the rod. It is advisable to remove any other objects that could make contact with the rod, such as rings or bracelets. If a ring cannot be removed cover it with surgical tape.

Select a sample of the desired substance, large enough to be kept in contact with the rod but small enough to be comfortable in the hand. The size of a plum stone is ideal. Clasp the sample in one hand by placing it in the centre of the palm and hold the rod so that the handle is in contact with the sample but still free to move. The rods should then react only to the same substance as the sample.

A simple way of testing this is in the road outside your own house. Most houses are connected to several utility services – water, gas, electricity, telephone – and most of these run below ground level, though electricity and telephone lines are sometimes overhead. Sewage is predominantly water. Pick one of these for your experiment – gas for example. Water is best left for the moment, as the powerful influence of the water may overshadow the influence of the pipe that carries it.

Dowse over the area without a sample and determine the reactions, which may cover all the services into the property. Now find which service responds to which reaction. It is easy to determine where the water pipe enters the property as there is usually a valve cover in the footpath; the sewer is in line with a manhole cover, and the line of the gas and electricity services can be guessed from the entry points inside the house.

To check which of these reactions is the gas pipe, a sample must be carried of the same material as the pipe. If the property dates from before 1970, the pipe will most probably be of steel. If it is newer, the pipe could be of plastic. First check this by examining the entry of the gas pipe into the house; the pipe before the cock will be the same as the buried one.

If the pipe is of steel, hold a piece of steel in the hand as a sample. A nut will do. It should be in contact with the rod as already described. Walk over the ground in the area where you believe the pipe to lie. You should get a clear and positive reaction over the gas pipe. You may also get a strong reaction over the water main, particularly if the water is flowing. It is advisable therefore to shut off all the taps in the house. (The contrary will apply when dowsing for your water pipe. Then a tap should be left on: a trickle will suffice.) Sampling will not work if you are using secondary handles.

If you have determined with reasonable accuracy the run of the pipe you have chosen to find, you are learning to divine. This experiment can then be repeated for the other services using different samples for the different services, the samples being of the same substance as the service sought. Some dowsers carry a small bag or box full of samples: small pieces of cable, iron, copper, lead, and so on. In the field you can experiment with minerals such as iron (it is surprising how many pieces of old iron lie buried) and copper.

A rod was once marketed which had several samples attached to one handle on a length of thread, like a string of beads. The dowser would hold the sample required, the samples being separated by an inch or so of thread. This was an appealing but cumbersome refinement.

Sampling for water is unnecessary, as one quickly learns to recognise a reaction to this most powerful of influences, but it can be done if you want by using a very small bottle or phial, an old scent bottle for example, filled with clean water and stoppered with a real cork. Artificial bungs of rubber or plastic will not work. Hold the phial in the usual way for sampling, but with the cork in contact with the handle of the rod.

3. Other methods of dowsing

The bent metal rod is an ideal introduction to the art of dowsing. However, there are more interesting and satisfying methods.

A troublesome drawback with metal rods is that they become too sensitive as the dowser becomes more accomplished. It can be tiresome if the rods react to sundry items which are of little or no interest. For example, when searching for something specific such as a water pipe, it is confusing to the search if one continually also discovers buried stones, scrap metal and the like. Bent metal rods also have an unnatural feel to them. Being man-made, they seem to intrude in the natural world.

The twig

The twig is the traditional dowser's rod, and it is referred to as a twig to distinguish it from bent metal rods. It has several advantages over any other method. It is a tool available at all times throughout the year and can be found in any hedgerow or wood. It is a natural material and with usage the dowser develops a strong affinity to it. It is much less sensitive than the metal rods as it reacts only to stronger influences, and so the dowser is freed from having to eliminate unimportant and unwanted reactions.

The type of tree or shrub is not important, but the twig chosen must be supple, easy to bend without breaking, but not so easy that it becomes limp in the hands. Young but not green wood is best, and last year's growth is preferable. Hazel, the traditional twig, is excellent, and its reputation as a good dowsing rod is fully justified. It also has a place in folklore, which enhances its prestige. However, any other twig with similar characteristics will do, such as beech, apple, privet, birch or willow. Brittle twigs, such as elder, pear or ash, are not satisfactory as they break easily.

The twig will last until it dries out and breaks, usually in seven days or so, depending on where it is stored and on the weather. A good dowsing twig is difficult to find and short-lived.

Cut a Y-shaped twig, the two branches being of as near equal girth as possible, with a diameter not exceeding 1 centimetre (3/8 inch). Each branch should be approximately 50 centimetres (20 inches) long, the stem not exceeding 10 centimetres (4 inches) (see Fig. 7). Examine the joint and make certain that it is not damaged, as many are. A weak joint will snap easily under stress. Avoid choosing a twig with branches of large diameter, as these take considerable strength to handle and are therefore very tiring to the user. If the branches are too thin the twig will be too supple and will be unwieldy in the hands. If the diameters of the branches are greatly dissimilar, the whole twig will have a strong bias to one side, difficult and sometimes impossible to correct. Avoid green, dead, diseased or damaged wood. Leave the bark on. This makes

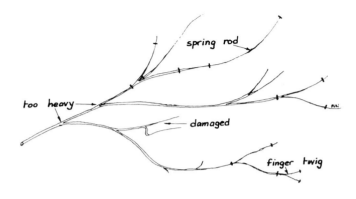

7. How to cut suitable dowsing twigs from a branch.

no difference to the dowser, except that freshly stripped twigs are wet and sticky.

Finding a twig which conforms to all these requirements is not an easy task. It will take a considerable amount of delving into the undergrowth and hedgerows to find the perfect twig. Remove the twig from the plant without damaging either. The use of a sharp knife, rather than snapping the branch, leaves a tidy plant and makes for a tidy twig. One is less likely to incur the wrath of the farmer if twigs are removed with care.

Dress the twig by removing all the leaves and lesser branches with care. Again a sharp knife is recommended.

Using the twig

The method of holding the twig is difficult to learn, and until one is fully familiar with it, it is advisable to follow a set procedure.

First hold the ends of the branches, one in each hand. Grip these firmly and place your thumbs on the wood, not round the twig or over the cut ends. The thumbs should both point to the sky, the point of the twig towards the ground. As most twigs have unequal branches to some extent, the stronger branch should be held in the stronger hand. The forearms should be horizontal, with the

8. Dowsing with a twig. The thumbs must point outwards and the palms of the hands must face upwards.

elbows tucked into the sides of the body.

Next, turn both hands simultaneously by twisting the wrists, so that the thumbs point outwards and the point of the twig points away from the body. The palms of the hands should now be facing the sky; if they do not, the position is incorrect and the procedure must be repeated. The twig and the forearms should be in the same horizontal plane. The elbows should still be tucked into the sides of the body.

Now flex the twig by widening and narrowing the gap between the fists to create a tension within the twig. This takes practice, and by trial and error you should aim to create a state of equilibrium in the twig so that it could rise or fall at the slightest provocation. It may be necessary to try different twigs of varying lengths and diameters and to hold the twig in different places until the correct combination is found.

Finally, when you have found your ideal twig and you have it in a state of tense equilibrium, you are ready to walk the ground.

Follow the same procedure as described for the bent metal rods. The reaction will be a raising or lowering of the point. Maintain your grip at all times. Sometimes considerable strength is required to hold the twig and to prevent it from wrenching itself from the hands. This has a profound effect on the novice, who is astonished by the amount of force exerted by the twig.

The twig will rise for some, the stem pointing upwards; for others it will fall, the stem pointing downwards. There is no significance in this. It is the dowsing equivalent to left and right handedness but is not related to it. Bent metal rods swing inwards (most usually) or outwards for the same reason. When a very strong reaction is encountered, the twig may turn by as much as 180 degrees, until the stem is pointing at the body. The strength required to hold such a reacting twig is so great that it is not unknown for the bark to peel off in the hands.

Unlike the metal rods, the twig does not correct itself, except occasionally when minor reactions are encountered which deflect the twig by a small amount, about 10 degrees from the horizontal.

Eventually the rod will become unusable through drying out. However, the novice dowser will soon find which type of twig suits him best and the ideal size and diameter for him.

Finger twigs and whalebone

Some people enjoy greater success with finger twigs, so called because they are miniature versions of the larger twigs held in the fingers.

Cut a small twig, with branches of about 15 centimetres (6 inches) in length and a stem less than 3 centimetres (1¼ inches). Hold the branches between the first finger and thumb of each hand with the thumb nails facing skyward and pointing away from

9. The twig reacts by raising or lowering and may turn by as much as 180 degrees so that it points towards the dowser.

the body. Finger twigs are quite sensitive and are especially useful for children and people with arthritic hands and wrists.

For those who prefer a permanent twig, whalebone may be used. Procure two whalebones approximately 50 centimetres (20 inches) long. These are obtainable, with some difficulty, from certain dressmakers and corsetiers. Lay them together, broad sides touching, and bind one end only with strong thread. This should be done very tightly so that the rods are secured. The resultant instrument resembles a twig and is used in the same way, but it has an indefinite life.

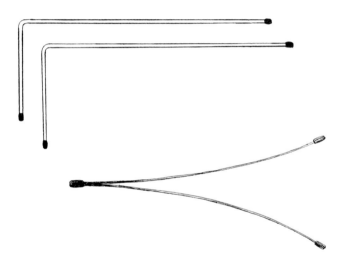

10. *A forked spring steel rod and plastic-covered steel angle rods are marketed as part of a detecting kit (see page 37).*

The pendulum

The pendulum is favoured by many dowsers, especially professionals. For those who can use it successfully, it provides a different concept of dowsing because of its flexibility.

The pendulum can be made of any material but wood is preferable and the string should be of natural fibre. You can either make one for yourself or have one made by a wood turner. As a refinement it can be hollowed and plugged to form a receptacle for samples. As an experiment the dowser might try using a cotton

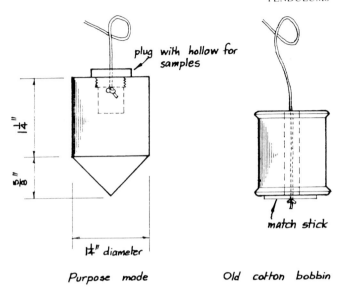

plug with hollow for samples

$1\frac{1}{4}''$

$\frac{5}{8}''$

$1\frac{1}{4}''$ diameter

Purpose made

match stick

Old cotton bobbin

11. Home-made pendulums.

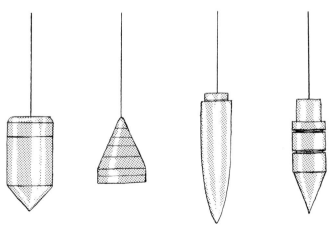

12. Solid and cavity pendulums can be bought in a range of shapes.

23

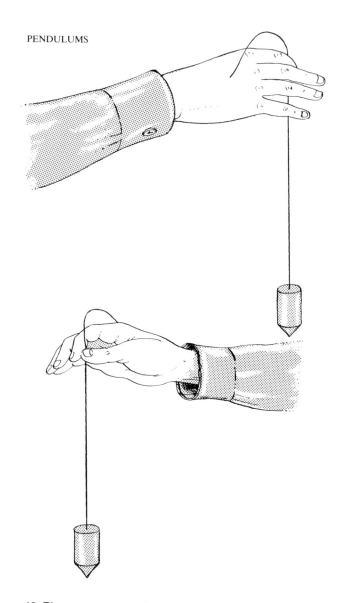

13. *The correct way to hold a pendulum.*

14. The pendulum reacts by oscillating and ultimately by gyrating.

bobbin (one of the old wooden ones is better than a recent plastic one).

The pendulum is very versatile and the most portable of all dowsing devices. The shape should be similar to a child's spinning top or a plumb-bob, having a rounded body pointed at the bottom and flat on the top, with a length of string either attached to the top or passing through a central hole. It should look roughly like the one shown above.

The string should be held between the forefinger and thumb of one hand, the writing hand. The thumb and forefinger should form a circle. The other fingers should fan out facing the ground.

With the pendulum hanging freely from his hand and with his arm stretched out comfortably, the dowser should walk the ground slowly until the pendulum starts to oscillate. The one disadvantage of the pendulum in the field is that a wind as light as a breeze will have the same effect, so a calm day should be chosen. The dowser must then stand still. The pendulum will continue to oscillate, the arc of sweep increasing until it converts the oscillation into a gyration.

The various strengths of the reactions will determine how large the arc of sweep is when oscillating and the height to which the pendulum will climb when gyrating. Different dowsers have different ways of reading pendulums, and a science has grown up surrounding this strange instrument.

One method is to calibrate a table by experimentation. This is done by relating the length of the string to the substance found. The dowser must divine for known substances and measure the length of string held in the hand, for it will be found that the pendulum will react only when the string is of the correct length for the substance.

Another method is to calibrate the number of clockwise and anticlockwise gyrations of the pendulum, should it have clear starting and finishing points. The lengths of string and the gyrations vary from person to person and each chart of calibrations is unique to the user.

Many people cannot use a pendulum, so the novice should not be too disappointed if his results are negative. For those who can use it, it is a most rewarding tool. Sampling can be done as before, the sample being in contact with the string or, alternatively, placed in the hollow of the bob.

Spring rod

Spring rods can be of wood, whalebone or spring steel. If made of wood, it should be from the tips of a branch and must be very supple indeed, very thin and about 30 centimetres (12 inches) long. Whalebone should be the standard corsetry type, and an old clock spring will suffice for a spring rod of steel.

The rod should be grasped in the hands, thumbs pointing inwards, each hand holding one end of the rod. The rod must be placed in tension by making it form a loop similar to a pig's tail (see below).

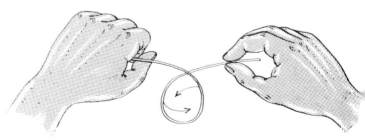

15. The correct way to hold a spring rod.

The reaction to look for is the loop moving along the rod noticeably or turning over completely. It is reminiscent of the movement of a snake. The rod will react and reset itself as the dowser walks the ground. It is a method favoured by many well known dowsers.

Other methods

There are several other methods of dowsing, sometimes of a complicated nature, sometimes bizarre, sometimes manufactured. The amateur could progress to these if he chooses. However, he will obtain all the excitement of dowsing by using the methods already described and at little or no cost.

A very few gifted people are so sensitive that they can dowse using an open hand held palm downwards. They feel a tingling sensation of varying intensity in the hand and fingers. You may be one of these rare people!

16. Scanning with a pendulum.

4. Some advanced techniques

Scanning

To avoid the chore of searching an area metre by metre, zig-zagging over an entire field, the dowser can use the method of scanning.

Using the pendulum, stand at one edge of the search area. With the free arm, fingers closed together, make a very slow sweep of the area, similar to the movement of a very slow windscreen wiper. Holding a long stick will increase your sensitivity. Check the pendulum for a reaction, no matter how slight. Stop the sweep and allow the pendulum to carry through its reaction, exactly as described for normal dowsing. With the help of an assistant mark the position in which the dowser is standing and mark a point across the field exactly in line with the sweeping arm.

Move to one side of the first position so that you are at right angles to the first scan and repeat the procedure.

Now imagine a line joining the first two markers and another joining the second two markers. Determine an approximate position where these two imaginary lines might intersect. By walking the ground within this smaller area, using one of the conventional dowsing techniques, you will find the exact location of the reaction.

Scanning can also be undertaken by some people using bent metal rods. When the dowser is walking the ground, both rods may move together but parallel to each other. The rods appear to be pointing. Follow the direction thus suggested until the rods react normally.

These techniques require refinement but they can be improved upon with practice. They will save you much time in searching and greatly reduce the distance you need to walk. This is very useful for dowsing can be an extremely tiring pastime.

Assessing depth and quantity

It is usually found that a strong influence, such as water or a mineral vein, will give more than one reaction. The novice dowser will find, after much practice, that differing degrees of reaction will become evident. This is most marked with bent metal rods, which will show great variation, from crossing (or opening) a little, through several stages until they cross (or open) completely. With the twig the dip or rise will vary from a little to a full swing of up to 180 degrees. This will be evident in a pattern, which will reverse itself.

For instance, when you are walking over an influence it will

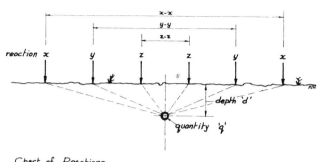

Chart of Reactions

distances		deflection	depth 'd'	quantity 'q'
x-x	14m	10°	6m	10 g.p.m. (·76 L/s)
y-y	10m	30°		
z-z	5m	80°		
x-x	16m	10°	7·5m	20 g.p.m. (1·5 L/s)
y-y	8m	40°		
z-z	2m	90°		
x-x	6m	15°	1m	25 g.p.m. (1·9L/s)
y-y	3m	45°		
z-z	1m	180°		

17. A table of reactions based upon the degree of deflection of the twig or rods can pinpoint the position and depth of the object.

become apparent that there are several reactions, which start weakly and strengthen, then weaken again. It will also be noted that there are two reactions which are stronger than the rest. The source of the influence will lie halfway between these two strongest reactions. Reactions immediately above a source are unusual.

The distance between the two weakest reactions should be measured, and half of this distance is the approximate depth of the influence. This is commonly known as the Bishop's Rule, named after a French cleric who is believed to have originated the theory.

Some dowsers claim to be able to determine, in the case of water, the direction of flow and the quantity. The former can be guessed by the lie of the land and some elementary knowledge of geology. Water always flows downhill below the ground, as it does above it.

Determining quantity is learnt only by long experience. Most professional dowsers can discriminate between reactions with barely perceptible differences. These differences are important for they can reveal the unseen and convey both depth and quantity. A dowser of great ability and experience can with conviction not only point to the site of a proposed well but can also give the depth of the water within ten per cent and an impression of quantity.

The amateur, by careful experimentation, can draw up a table, based on his own particular reactions. To do this, he must know of several sources of flowing water of known depth: the water main into the house, a street sewer, and so on. Dowse these carefully, marking the points of reaction, and note the degree of response. This is the deflection in degrees from the normal position, that is vertical deflection of the twig and horizontal deflection of the rods. A picture can thus be built up consisting of ground distances and deflection set against depths and quantities. These can be tabulated in the form of a graph, as illustrated opposite.

It is not difficult to ascertain the flow rate of water by measurement and calculation. Remember that the tap must be turned on, and the discharge rate can be measured by timing the filling of a bucket of known capacity. If, for example, it takes twelve seconds to fill a 2-gallon bucket, this is equal to 12 gallons per minute. The flow rate of the tap can be altered to give a range of flow rates with consequent differences in dowsing reactions.

This experiment can be repeated at different premises, having differing depths of water mains. The help of friends with this is invaluable.

5. If you are not successful

Autosuggestion

It is easy to be carried away with your own enthusiasm, particularly when you are new to the art. The familiarity of use can encourage the would-be dowser to cause spurious reactions of his own making. This can become a serious problem and is difficult to eliminate. The popular way of overcoming autosuggestion is to check your findings by suggesting to yourself that the rods should not move. If you concentrate on this and repeat to yourself 'do not react' and the rods then stop working, there is a possibility that the reaction was the product of your own subconscious. Alternatively, get a fellow dowser to check the reactions independently. Guard against overstressing the matter, for the opposite might occur. The ideal way of checking is to use the services of a friend who can dowse, but clearly he should not be a witness to your dowsing.

Failure

Should the novice, after trying repeatedly, fail to dowse, there are several points for him to consider and try.

You may be trying too hard. Many a would-be dowser has suffered the disappointment of failure, only because he wished too ardently to do it. This probably explains why children are better than adults, for they have fewer inhibitions. It is easy to suggest a more relaxed approach, difficult to put it into practice, but this is what is needed.

You may be trying the wrong method. Very few people can use all the methods that have been described. Some people are excellent when using a pendulum and useless when trying to use rods. Try all the methods suggested.

Tiredness, illness, worry, or any distraction such as an audience can prevent one from dowsing.

Freedom of movement is important. A tight garment, rucksack or such like can impede possible reactions.

A dull overcast day, twilight or bad light of any sort can affect the dowser adversely. It is impossible to dowse in the dark or when blindfolded. Some dowsers prefer a sunny day and choose to face the sun.

Reactions may improve when natural leather shoes are worn, and some people prefer bare feet.

But if you have tried many times without success then you will have to accept that you are one of the very few who cannot dowse.

6. Other applications

So far, conventional applications of dowsing have been covered but, as might be expected, people have adapted the art for uses other than looking for material things such as water and minerals.

Good or bad

It is claimed by some that a dowser can ascertain whether a substance is good or bad, healthy or ill, compatible or not. The pendulum is the usual medium and is assumed to give positive or good reactions and negative or bad reactions. Some practitioners determine the suitability of soils for sowing, the seat of diseased tissue in the body, the discovery of tooth decay, the suitability of food, and so on. The Chinese are using pendulums for sexing chickens, apparently with considerable success.

These dowsers use touch for communication, by holding the pendulum in one hand and touching the substance in question with a finger of the other hand. Sometimes a wooden pointer is used.

This approach to dowsing is of interest to the novice but could be misleading and is possibly unwise in connection with medical matters.

Ley lines

A belief held by many is that our remote ancestors erected monoliths, henges and the like in a fixed pattern, linked by long straight lines called ley lines. These supposed lines are invisible and traverse miles across the countryside over hills, rivers, woods and fields. A new interest has grown up in seeking these lines on maps and checking them in the field. But this is a controversial belief, rejected by most historians.

Some dowsers claim that these lines follow certain 'earth forces', which cause strong dowsing reactions. It is further claimed that our ancestors could lay these lines of force themselves, thus enabling them to form the long straight tracks, some of which the Romans took over and improved.

One can certainly find some interesting and surprising reactions in and near to stone circles and standing stones. This subject is worthy of further experiment and research.

Map dowsing

Certain dowsers can operate on a site even though they are not present there. They do this by using a map of the area of search. This sounds incredible, but it has been proved to work. Outstanding finds have been made by dowsers, sometimes many miles from the area in question.

The pendulum already described is used, together with a pointer and compass. The pointer should be of a wood – a cocktail stick is ideal – and the compass should be an accurate magnetic type.

The best maps for the purpose are the 6 inches to the mile Ordnance Survey. Maps of a smaller scale are not so good as less detail is shown and the plotting of reactions may cover adjacent features.

Lay the map flat on a table at home. There is no need to be within the area under investigation. Using the compass, set the map to magnetic north, not forgetting to adjust the map to compensate for magnetic variation, which is explained on the 1:50,000 Ordnance Survey maps.

With the pendulum in the stronger hand and the pointer in the other, scan the map very slowly for the substance sought. The search should be carried out as described in chapter 4, with the pendulum held over the map and the pointer used to locate the source of reactions. It must always be borne in mind that this type of dowsing is a greatly scaled-down version of walking the ground. It should therefore be carried out very slowly indeed, and with great care and patience. Checking must be carried out conventionally in the field.

Some astonishing finds have been made using this method, including a claim, later proved, of finding water in a Middle Eastern desert region, by a dowser operating from England!

7. Conclusion

There are no strict rules for dowsing. People differ in their approach, attitude and interpretations. Practice will reveal the personal characteristics of each dowser, which will not vary greatly from dowser to dowser.

The ancients probably treated dowsing as a normal part of everyday living, using it as a tool with many valuable applications to their way of life. It is part of a sense lost to modern man and worthy of rediscovery. The evolution of technology from Roman times and religious disapproval have reduced dowsing to the level of a curiosity. Now a resurgence of interest is reviving the art, and the reader is encouraged to try dowsing and to enjoy the pastime for the pleasure it can bring.

Dowsing is now being taken seriously by several governmental organisations, some of which employ dowsers. The professional dowser is in demand again, not so much at village level but at national level. During the Vietnam war, United States Army engineers were trained to dowse for land mines. They proved to be more accurate than the conventional electronic detectors. The Soviet government has undertaken serious research into dowsing and has published interesting and convincing reports.

So dowsing does work, but how it works is a question as yet unanswered.

Many theories have been put forward, the strongest of which is the theory of the 'earth force', which is interpreted by some as an abstract name for the earth's magnetic field, which flows beneath the earth's surface and is changed in character slightly by obstacles in its path. This minute change is the earth force that dowsers react to. The rod or twig is a vehicle to convey the person's reaction, the muscles of the wrist being the prime mover. Those who argue that the wrist is turning and not the rods have missed the point.

This is a simplification for the layman of a complicated scientific phenomenon. It would certainly explain why only buried matter can be dowsed and why denser matter dowses more strongly than lighter matter. It could also account for the exhaustion felt by most dowsers after an hour or two of ostensibly light work.

The earth force theory can be extended to other unexplained phenomena. For example, it might have a bearing on how birds and mammals migrate, find water in deserts, pick specific routes across barren land, choose unlikely places for giving birth, and so on.

For the newcomer, a whole new world will be revealed, waiting to be explored beneath his feet. He will never look at the world with quite the same eyes again.

Further reading

Below is a very brief list of books on the subject. Those marked *
are available from the British Society of Dowsers. The remainder
are believed to be out of print but may be available on loan from
your local library or through the inter-library loan service. Certain
titles may be available second-hand from the Society of
Metaphysicians.

Those with access to the internet will find many sites dealing
with all forms of dowsing and divining. There are treatises which
relate the skill to the works of the devil and those which offer a
scientific explanation. These sites provide much food for thought
and the reader is encouraged to surf the web on the subject. Just
insert *dowsing* or *divining* into the search window and see what
you come up with!

Barrett, Sir William, and Besterman, Theodore. *The Divining Rod*.
University Books, 1968.

Bird, Christopher. *The Divining Hand*.* Whitford, USA, 1993.

Davies, Rodney. *Dowsing*. Aquarian Press, 1991.

Devereux, Paul. *The New Ley-hunter's Companion*.* Gothic Im-
age, 1993.

France, Henry de. *Elements of Dowsing*. Bell, 1948; reprinted 1977.

Graves, Tom. *The Diviner's Handbook*. Thorsons, 1986.

Graves, Tom. *The Dowser's Handbook*. Thorsons, 1989.

Graves, Tom. *Discover Dowsing*. Harper Collins, 1989.

Graves, Tom. *The Elements of Pendulum Dowsing*.* Element Books,
1989; reprinted 1997.

Lethbridge, T. C. *The Power of the Pendulum*.* Arkana, 1985.

Mermet, Abbé. *Principles and Practice of Radiesthesia*. Reprinted
by Element Books, 1987.

Ross, T. Edward, and Wright, Richard. *The Divining Mind*.* Des-
tiny Books, 1990.

Weaver, Herbert. *Divining the Primary Sense*. Routledge & Kegan
Paul, 1978.

Whitlock, Ralph. *Water Divining and Other Dowsing*. David &
Charles, 1982.

Organisations and equipment

The British Society of Dowsers: National Dowsing Centre, 2 St Anne's Road, Malvern, Worcestershire WR14 4RG. Telephone/fax: 01684 576969. Email: info@britishdowsers.org Website: www.britishdowsers.org This is the only organisation available for the dowser, amateur or professional. Membership is open to anyone who accepts the objects of the society.

The following organisations deal with the medical aspects of dowsing:

The Radionic Association, Baerlein House, Goose Green, Deddington, Banbury, Oxfordshire OX15 0SZ. Telephone: 01869 338852. Email: secretary@radionic.co.uk Website: www.radionic.co.uk A society for those interested in Radiesthesia etc.

The Society of Metaphysicians, Archer's Court, Stonestile Lane, The Ridge, Hastings, East Sussex TN35 4PG. Telephone: 01424 751577. Fax: 01424 722387. Email: newmeta@btinternet.com Website: www.newmeta.btinternet.co.uk

Bruce Copen Laboratories Limited, 4 Lindfield Enterprise Park, Lindfield, West Sussex RH16 2LX. Telephone: 01444 487900. Fax: 01444 483555. Email: info@copen.com Website: www.copen.com Specialists in Radiesthesia, radionics etc.

Index

Advanced techniques 29–31
Agricola, *De Re Metallica* 5
Assessing finds 29–31
Attitudes for dowsing 9, 18–20
Autosuggestion, adverse
    effects 32

Calibrating pendulum 26
Chinese use 5, 33
Church attitude 5, 35
Commercially produced rods
    14

Definition 5
Degrees of reaction 29, 30
Depth 30
De Re Metallica 4, 5
Determining results 14–16
Divinable elements 5
Divining 14, 15
Dowsing 12

Egyptian dowsers 5
Experimenting 12–15

Failure, reasons for 32
Finger twigs 20
Flow rate of water 31
French references 5

Hazel twig 6, 17
Heredity 6
Holding finger rod 20–1
    metal rod 9–12
    pendulum 24–5
    spring rod 26
    twig 19–20
Homemade rods 8, 9, 17, 18, 20

Influencing the rod 14–16
Interpreting results 14

Ley lines 33

Making metal rod 7–8
    pendulum 22–3
    twig 17, 18, 20, 21
    whalebone twig 22
Map dowsing 33
Medical dowsing 33
Metal rod dowsing 9–16
Misconceptions 6
Modern applications 6, 7, 35
Movement of pendulum 25
    metal rod 12
    spring rod 21
    twig 20, 21
Mullins family 6

Pendulum 22–6
Plotting reactions 12, 13
Purpose of dowsing 5, 6

Quantity of find 31

Reactions: metal rod 12
    pendulum 25
    spring rod 27
Reasons for failure 32
Rods 6, 8, 9

Sampling 14–16, 26
Scanning 28, 29
Spring rods 26, 27

Thouvenal 5
Twig dowsing 17–21

Vallemont, de 5

Whalebone twig 22
Where to dowse 9

SHIRE 'DISCOVERING' BOOKS

The 'Discovering' series includes the titles that are listed below together with their series numbers. Most of them are uniform with this book, but those marked with an asterisk are in the larger 'handbook' format, 210 by 128 mm. A free catalogue listing all 'Discovering' and other Shire books currently available, with their prices, may be obtained from Shire Publications.

* Discovering Abbeys and Priories (57) *Geoffrey N. Wright*
* Discovering Antique Prints (266) *Ronald Russell*
  Discovering Archaeology in England and Wales (46) *James Dyer*
  Discovering Backgammon (201) *R. C. Bell*
* Discovering Battlefields of England and Scotland (287) *John Kinross*
  Discovering Bells and Bellringing (29) *John Camp*
  Discovering Book Collecting (267) *John Chidley*
  Discovering British Military Badges and Buttons (148) *R. J. Wilkinson-Latham*
* Discovering British Regimental Traditions (292) *Ian F. W. Beckett*
  Discovering Cameras 1945–1965 (286) *Robert White*
  Discovering Canals in Britain (257) *Peter L. Smith*
* Discovering Cathedrals (112) *David Pepin*
  Discovering Church Architecture (214) *Mark Child*
  Discovering Cottage Architecture (275) *Christopher Powell*
  Discovering Country Winemaking (249) *Daphne More*
  Discovering Dowsing and Divining (251) *Peter Naylor*
  Discovering English Architecture (244) *T. W. West*
* Discovering English County Regiments (294) *Ian F. W. Beckett*
  Discovering English Customs and Traditions (66) *Margaret Gascoigne*
  Discovering Epitaphs (144) *Geoffrey N. Wright*
* Discovering Famous Graves (288) *Lynn F. Pearson*
  Discovering the Folklore of Plants (74) *Margaret Baker*
* Discovering Friendly and Fraternal Societies (295) *Victoria Solt Dennis*
  Discovering Hallmarks on English Silver (38) *John Bly*
  Discovering Heraldry (250) *Jacqueline Fearn*
  Discovering Herbs (89) *Kay N. Sanecki*
  Discovering Highwaymen (94) *Russell Ash*
  Discovering Hill Figures (12) *Kate Bergamar*
  Discovering Horse Brasses (44) *John Vince*
  Discovering Horse-drawn Vehicles (284) *D. J. Smith*
* Discovering Local History (290) *David Iredale and John Barrett*
  Discovering London Ceremonial and Traditions (281) *Julian Paget*
* Discovering London for Families (293) *Peter Matthews*
* Discovering London Statues and Monuments (42) *Margaret Baker*
  Discovering London Street Names (225) *John Wittich*

* Discovering London's Guilds and Liveries (180) *John Kennedy Melling*

Discovering Off-beat Walks in London (63) *John Wittich and Ron Phillips*

Discovering Oil Lamps (145) *Cecil A. Meadows*

Discovering Old Cameras 1839–1939 (260) *Robert White*

Discovering Old Handwriting (285) *John Barrett and David Iredale*

Discovering Parish Boundaries (282) *Angus Winchester*

* Discovering Prehistoric England (283) *James Dyer*

Discovering Preserved Railways (253) *F. G. Cockman*

Discovering the Ridgeway (211) *Vera Burden*

* Discovering Roman Britain (272) *David E. Johnston*

Discovering Saints in Britain (64) *John Vince*

Discovering Scottish Architecture (278) *T. W. West*

Discovering Stained Glass (43) *John Harries and Carola Hicks*

Discovering Surnames (35) *J. W. Freeman*

Discovering Timber-framed Buildings (242) *Richard Harris*

Discovering Traditional Farm Buildings (262) *J. E. C. Peters*

* Discovering Your Family Tree (93) *David Iredale and John Barrett*

* Discovering Your Old House (14) *David Iredale and John Barrett*